Labor Day

by Mari C. Schuh

Consulting Editor: Gail Saunders-Smith, Ph.D.

Consultant: Alexa Sandmann, Ed.D.
Professor of Literacy
The University of Toledo
Member, National Council for the Social Studies

Pebble Books

an imprint of Capstone Press
Mankato, Minnesota

Pebble Books are published by Capstone Press
151 Good Counsel Drive, P.O. Box 669, Mankato, Minnesota 56002
http://www.capstone-press.com

1 2 3 4 5 6 08 07 06 05 04 03

Library of Congress Cataloging-in-Publication Data
Schuh, Mari C., 1975–
    Labor Day / by Mari C. Schuh.
        p. cm.—(National holidays)
    Summary: Simple text and photographs describe the history of Labor Day and
how this holiday, which honors people who work, is celebrated in the United States.
    Includes bibliographical references and index.
    ISBN 0-7368-1653-4 (hardcover)
    1. Labor Day—Juvenile literature. [1. Labor Day. 2. Holidays.] I. Title.
II. Series.
HD7791.S37 2003
394.264—dc21   2002010032

Note to Parents and Teachers

The National Holidays series supports national social studies standards related to understanding events that celebrate the values and principles of American democracy. This book describes and illustrates Labor Day. The photographs support early readers in understanding the text. This book also introduces early readers to subject-specific vocabulary words, which are defined in the Words to Know section. Early readers may need assistance to read some words and to use the Table of Contents, Words to Know, Read More, Internet Sites, and Index/Word List sections of the book.

Table of Contents

Labor Day is a day
to honor people who work.

September						
S	M	T	W	T	F	S
	1	2	3	4	5	6
7	8	9	10	11	12	13
14	15	16	17	18	19	20
21	22	23	24	25	26	27
28	29	30				

6

Labor Day is on
the first Monday
in September. Labor Day
is right before many
schools start. It comes
at the end of summer.

IRON MOLDERS
UNION
No 14
PITTSBURG
ORGANISED
18

ARE THE
CHAINS
OF LIBERTY
BROKEN?

LIVE
AND
LET LIVE

8

Americans celebrated the first Labor Day in 1882.

10

President Grover Cleveland
made Labor Day
a national holiday
in 1894.

Most people do not go to work on Labor Day. Most offices and schools are closed on Labor Day.

Some cities have parades on Labor Day. Important people give speeches.

Many people have picnics on Labor Day. Some people go swimming.

Some people go camping
on Labor Day. Other
people visit parks.

Labor Day is a day
to honor people who work
hard all year. It is also
a day to relax.

Words to Know

American—someone who was born in the United States or is living in the United States

celebrate—to do something fun on a special day

holiday—a day to celebrate an event or to honor a person

honor—to show respect or to praise; Americans celebrate Labor Day to honor all people who work.

labor—to work

national—having to do with a country as a whole

parade—a line of people, bands, cars, and floats that travels through a town; parades celebrate special events and holidays.

picnic—a meal that is eaten outside, often at a park

relax—to rest and take it easy; many people relax on holidays.

Ansary, Mir Tamim. *Labor Day.* Holiday Histories. Des Plaines, Ill.: Heinemann Library, 1999.

Bredeson, Carmen. *Labor Day.* Rookie Read-About Holidays. New York: Children's Press, 2001.

Murphy, Patricia J. *Our National Holidays.* Our Nation. Minneapolis: Compass Point Books, 2002.

Internet Sites

Track down many sites about Labor Day.
Visit the FACT HOUND at *http://www.facthound.com*

IT IS EASY! IT IS FUN!

1) Go to *http://www.facthound.com*

2) Type in: 0736816534

3) Click on "FETCH IT" and FACT HOUND will find several links hand-picked by our editors.

Relax and let our pal FACT HOUND do the research for you!

Index/Word List

Word Count: 125
Early-Intervention Level: 12

Credits
Heather Kindseth, series designer; Molly Nei, book designer; Gene Bentdahl, illustrator; Karrey Tweten, photo researcher

Bettmann/Corbis, 8
Capstone Press/Jim Foell, 12
Comstock, Inc., 1, 6, 16 (both)
EyeWire Images, 18
Hulton Archive by Getty Images, 10
Index Stock Imagery/Lawrence Sawyer, 4
Larry Downing/Reuters/Corbis, 14
SW Productions/PhotoDisc, cover
Unicorn Stock Photos, 20